# MY E

**I BELONG TO:**

**PHONE NUMBER:**

**EMAIL:**

*If you find me please get in touch with my owner.*
*Thank you!*

*'I created this book to help enthusiasts capture insights, interpretations, & information acquired throughout their personal tarot journey, in one organized place.'*

# TAROT IS AN ART

If one hundred people were asked to draw a tree, there would be one hundred drawings of a tree. All different, yet all trees.

This is Claire's view of reading tarot cards.

Everyone brings their unique style of reading tarot cards: influenced by life skills, experiences, intuition, & learnings. Meanings that resonate with one person may not make sense to another. So, who is right? We all are!

Tarot is centuries old, with the definitions & keywords evolving over time. An example of this is the electronic age that was unheard of in the 15th century. Tarot continues to grow & adapt to the life in which we live.

There are correspondences that can be linked to tarot, like numerology & astrology.

Incorporating these into a tarot reading can add deeper, richer layers which are wonderful for the querent, but mean there is even more knowledge to retain for the reader.

'Tarot and Me' aims to keep all your information organized & in one place. It will become your personal reference guide that can be added to as you continue your tarot adventure.

Stay magical,

*Claire Lily xo*

www.claire-lily.com
www.tarotandme.com

# YOU GET TO DECIDE WHAT GOES INTO YOUR BOOK

*here are some correspondence ideas:-*

- upright
- reversed
- timing
- numerology
- astrology
- Kabbalah
- music
- phrases
- personal
- experience
- actor/ess
- characters in a show/tv/book
- family
- mind map
- angels
- colors
- lyrics
- own quotes
- others' quotes
- symbols
- Myers Briggs (great for Court Cards)
- deities
- animals
- plants
- crystals

# SECTIONS

- Major Arcana
- Minor Arcana
- Court Cards
- Spreads
- Card Combinations
- Tarot Decks
- Other Decks
- Books
- Podcasts
- Websites
- Social Media
- Courses
- Notes

# HOW TO USE YOUR BOOK

Don't feel like you must fill out every single page all at once!

Take your time & go at your own pace.

It doesn't matter which tarot deck, or decks you use.

This is a place to contain your creative tarot ideas & keep everything organized.

You'll be able to transfer any previous notes or scribbles straight into this one!

# 0

# THE FOOL

*A place for primary insights*

| Draw or print out your favorite 'Fool" card & paste it here | The number 0 - zero - a circle, There is no beginning & no end - all is possible. Both everything & nothing at the same time. No preconceived ideas or unlearning to do. |
|---|---|

I was 'The Fool' when...
I left England to be with my then-boyfriend after only 6 months of knowing him!

♫ The Fool on the Hill - The Beatles

★ new adventure
★ taking a risk
★ innocence
★ brand new journey
★ trusting the process

Reversals

Be aware of jumping in without thinking
Not quite ready

Do not fear mistakes. There are none!
Miles Davis

## Aquarius
January 23 - February 19

# A place to brainstorm

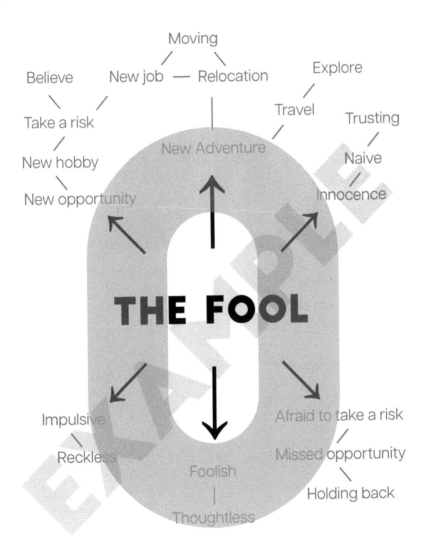

Moving

Believe — New job — Relocation — Explore

Take a risk — Travel — Trusting

New hobby — New Adventure — Naive

New opportunity — Innocence

# THE FOOL

Impulsive — Afraid to take a risk

Reckless — Missed opportunity

Foolish — Holding back

Thoughtless

# 0      THE FOOL

*A place to be creative. Use these two pages as you like!*

*How does the card make me feel?*

*What do I see?*

*What do I hear?*

# 0

# THE FOOL

*What does the dog mean to me in the card?*

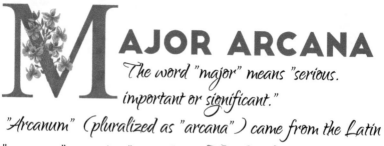

# MAJOR ARCANA

*The word "major" means "serious.*
*important or significant."*

*"Arcanum" (pluralized as "arcana") came from the Latin*
*"arcanus," meaning "secret," i.e "The Significant Secrets"*

# MAJOR ARCANA

# MAJOR ARCANA

# MAJOR ARCANA

# 0

# THE FOOL

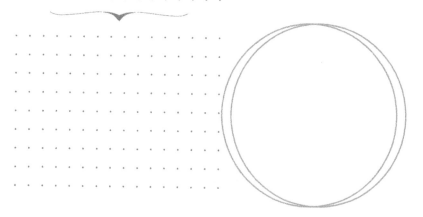

THE FOOL

# 0 THE FOOL

# 0 THE FOOL

# THE MAGICIAN

★
★
★
★
★

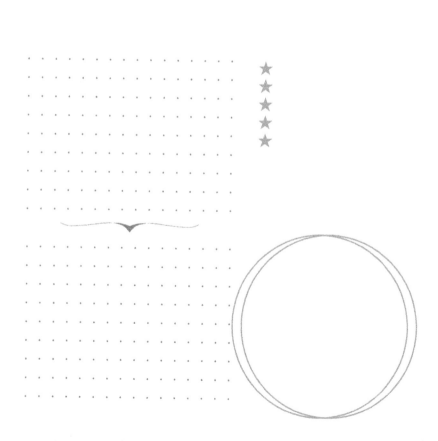

# THE MAGICIAN

# I THE MAGICIAN

# THE MAGICIAN

# 2 THE HIGH PRIESTESS

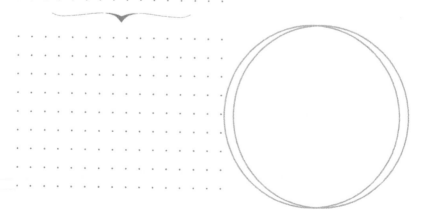

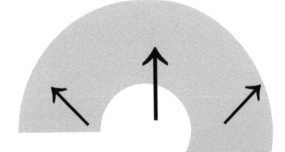

# THE HIGH PRIESTESS

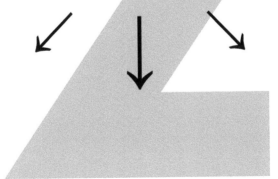

# 2 THE HIGH PRIESTESS

# 2 THE HIGH PRIESTESS

# **3** THE EMPRESS

★
★
★
★
★

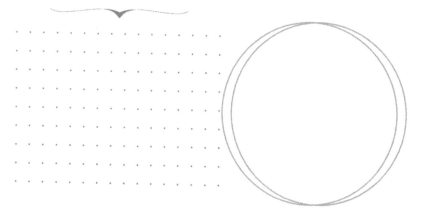

THE EMPRESS

# 3 THE EMPRESS

# 3  THE EMPRESS

# 4 THE EMPEROR

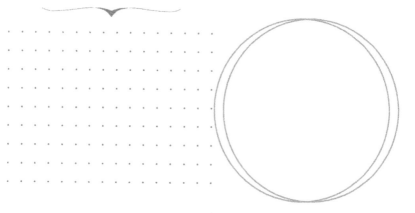

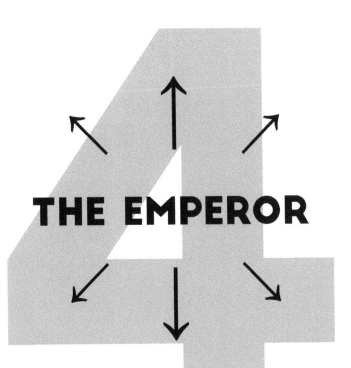

THE EMPEROR

# 4 THE EMPEROR

# 4 THE EMPEROR

# 5 THE HIEROPHANT

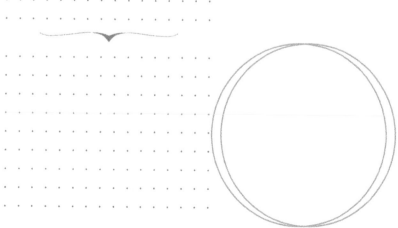

# THE HIEROPHANT

# 5 THE HIEROPHANT

# 5 THE HIEROPHANT

# 6 THE LOVERS

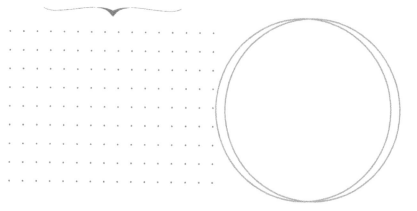

THE LOVERS

# 6 THE LOVERS

# 6 THE LOVERS

# 7 THE CHARIOT

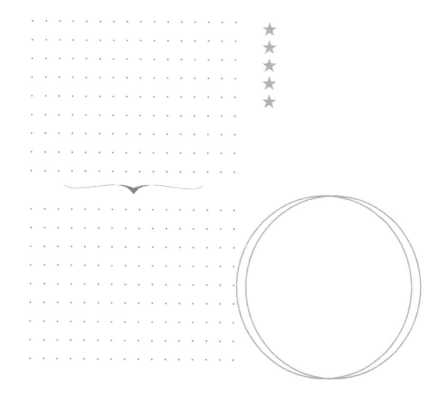

★
★
★
★
★

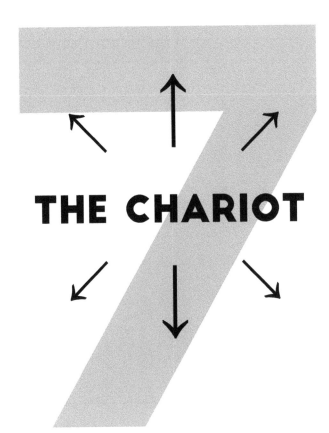

# THE CHARIOT

# 7 THE CHARIOT

# 7 THE CHARIOT

# 8 STRENGTH

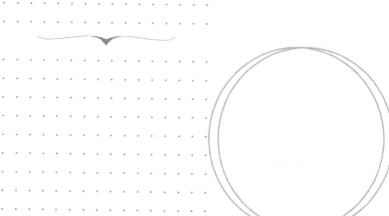

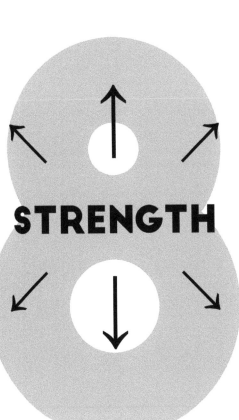

# 8 STRENGTH

# 8 STRENGTH

# 9 THE HERMIT

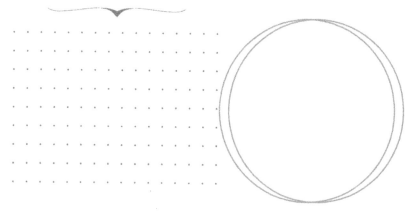

THE HERMIT

# 9 THE HERMIT

# 9    THE HERMIT

# 10 THE WHEEL OF FORTUNE

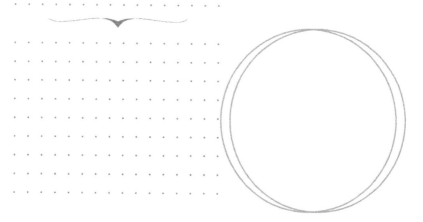

# THE WHEEL
# OF FORTUNE

# 10 THE WHEEL OF FORTUNE

# 10 THE WHEEL OF FORTUNE

# JUSTICE

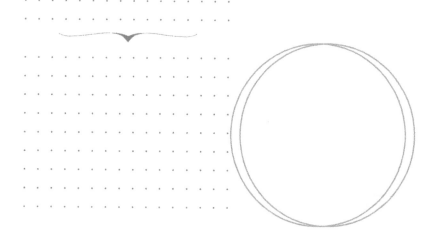

# 11 JUSTICE

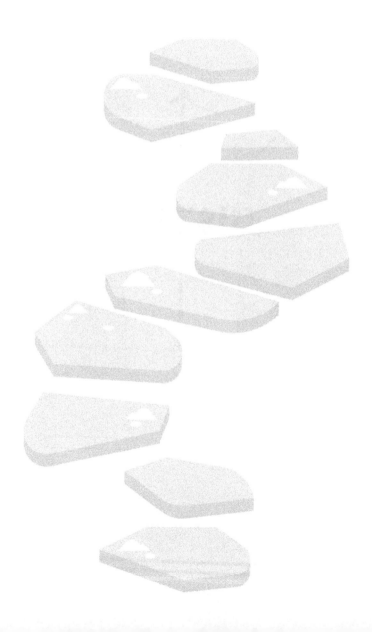

# 11

# JUSTICE

# 12 THE HANGED MAN

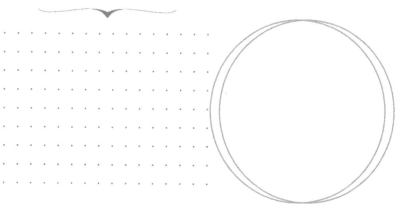

THE HANGED MAN

# 12 THE HANGED MAN

# 12 THE HANGED MAN

# 13 DEATH

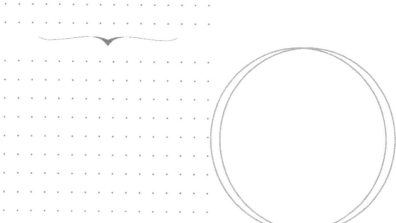

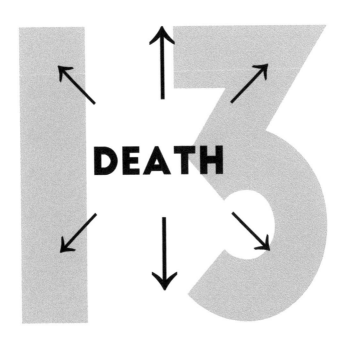

DEATH

# 13 DEATH

# 13

# DEATH

# 14 TEMPERANCE

★
★
★
★
★

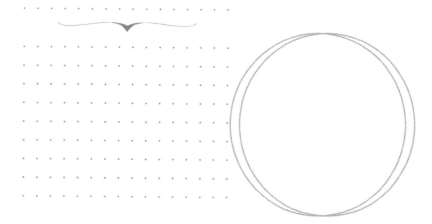

TEMPERANCE

# 14 TEMPERANCE

# 14 TEMPERANCE

# 15 THE DEVIL

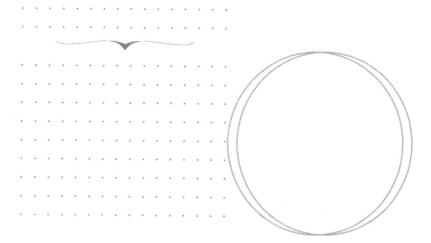

THE DEVIL

# 15 THE DEVIL

# 15 THE DEVIL

# 16 THE TOWER

★
★
★
★
★

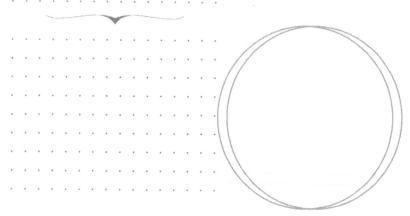

THE TOWER

# 16 THE TOWER

# 16 THE TOWER

# 17 THE STAR

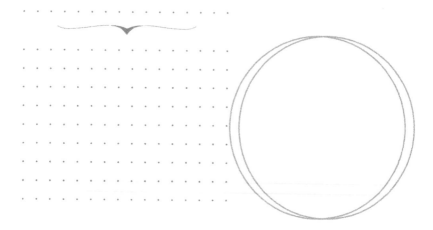

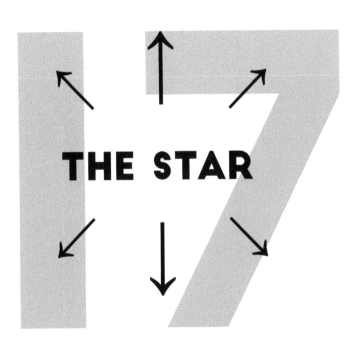

**THE STAR**

# 17 THE STAR

# 17 THE STAR

# 18 THE MOON

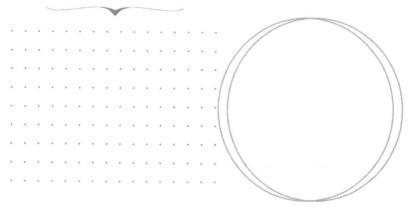

THE MOON

# 18 THE MOON

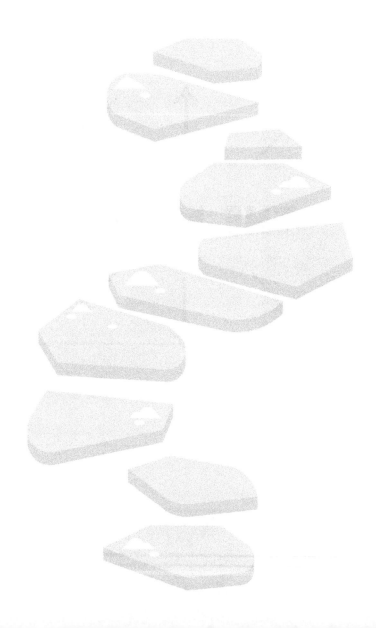

# 18 THE MOON

# 19 THE SUN

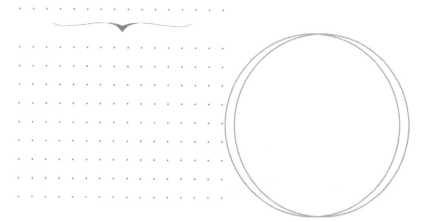

THE SUN

# 19 THE SUN

# 19 THE SUN

# 20 JUDGEMENT

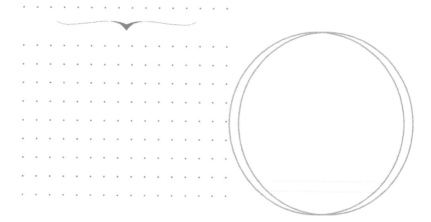

JUDGEMENT

# 20 JUDGEMENT

# 20 JUDGEMENT

# 21 THE WORLD

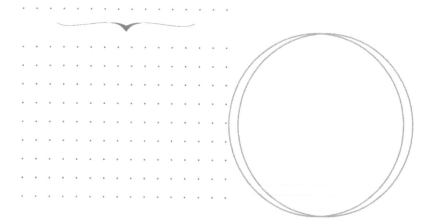

THE WORLD

# 21 THE WORLD

# 21 THE WORLD

# MINOR ARCANA

*The word "minor" can mean "lesser" "in important, seriousness or significance i.e "The Lesser Secrets"*

# MINOR ARCANA

# MINOR ARCANA

# MINOR ARCANA

# SUIT OF CUPS

*Other names include: Chalices, Goblets, Hearts*

# SUIT OF CUPS

# SUIT OF CUPS

# SUIT OF CUPS

# ACE OF CUPS

★
★★
★★★
★★★★
★★★★★

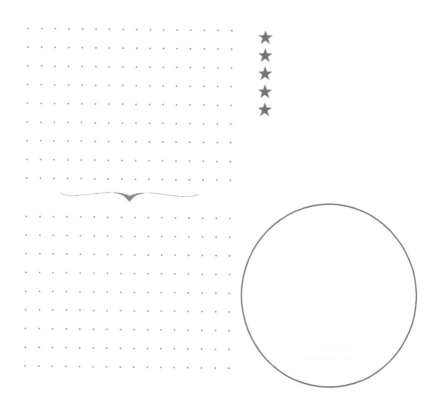

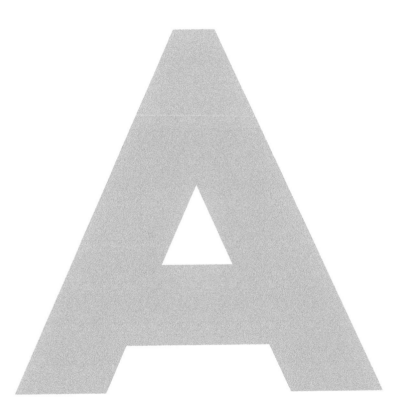

# TWO OF CUPS

★
★
★
★
★

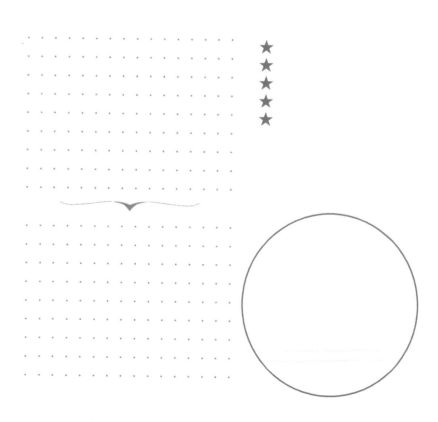

# THREE OF CUPS

★
★
★
★
★

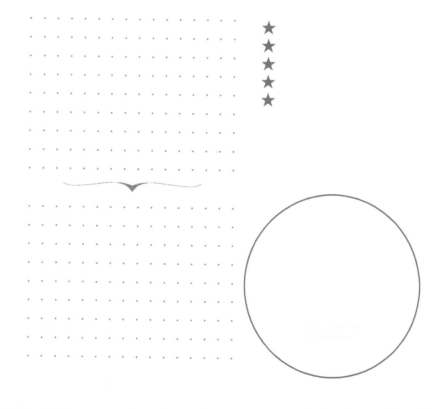

# FOUR OF CUPS

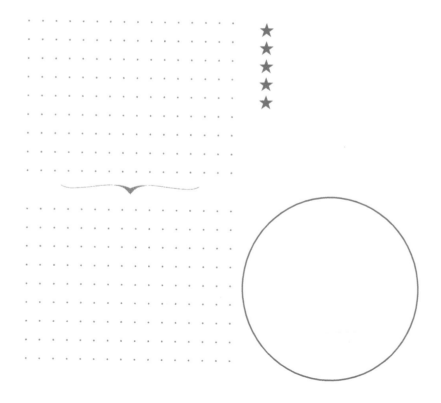

# FIVE OF CUPS

★
★
★
★
★

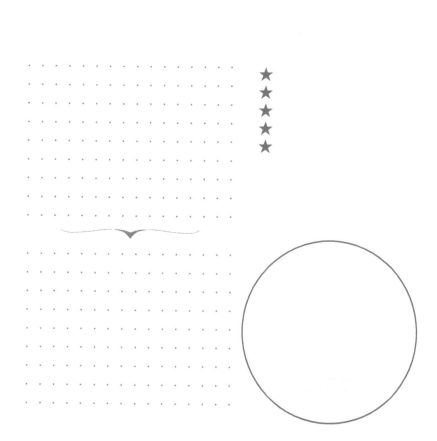

# SIX OF CUPS

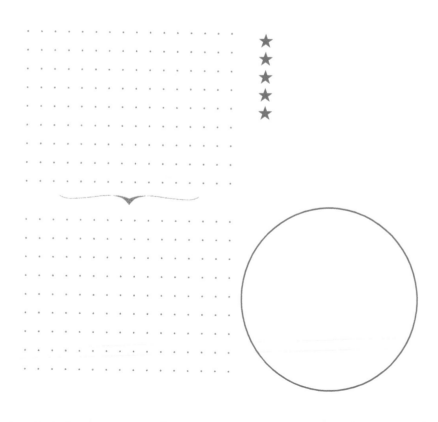

# SEVEN OF CUPS

★
★
★
★
★

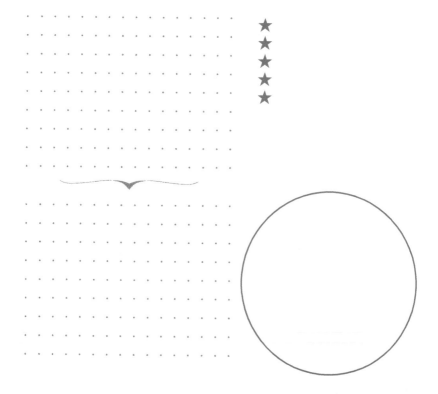

# EIGHT OF CUPS

★
★
★
★
★

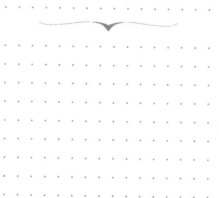

# NINE OF CUPS

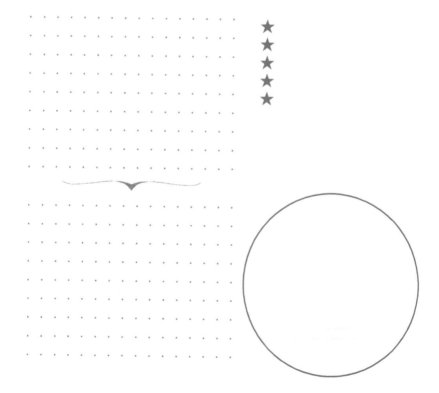

# TEN OF CUPS

★
★
★
★
★

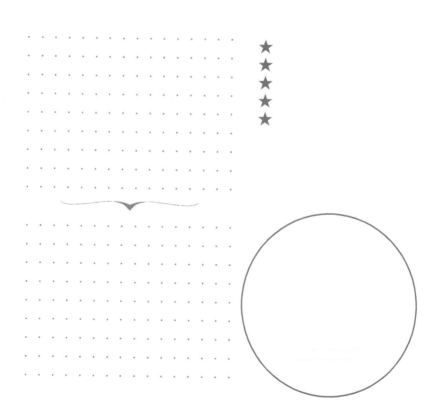

# SUIT OF PENTACLES

*Other names include: Coins, Discs, Diamonds*

# SUIT OF PENTACLES

# SUIT OF PENTACLES

# SUIT OF PENTACLES

# ACE OF PENTACLES

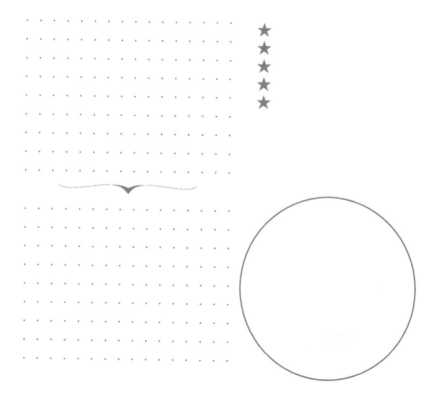

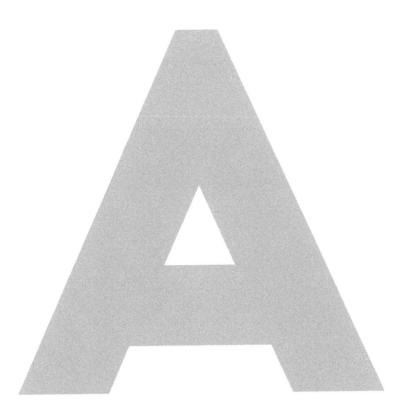

★
★
★
★
★

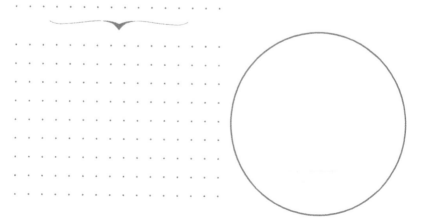

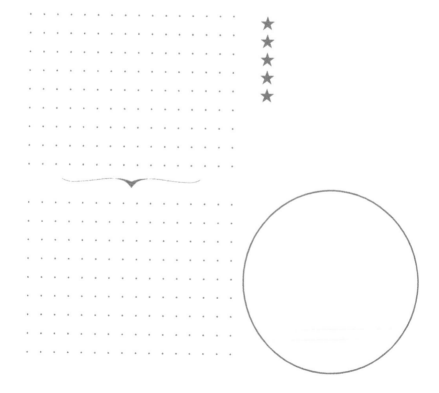

# FOUR OF PENTACLES

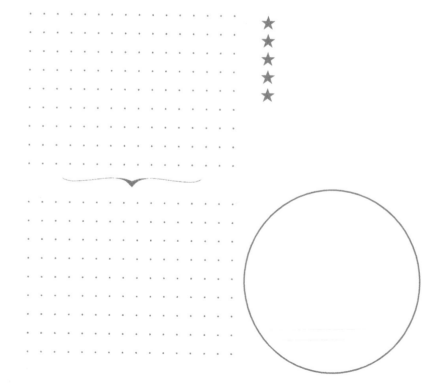

★
★
★
★
★

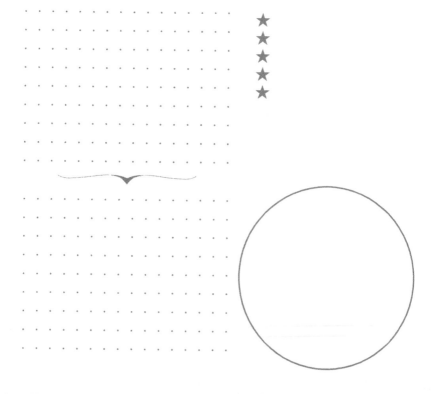

# SIX OF PENTACLES

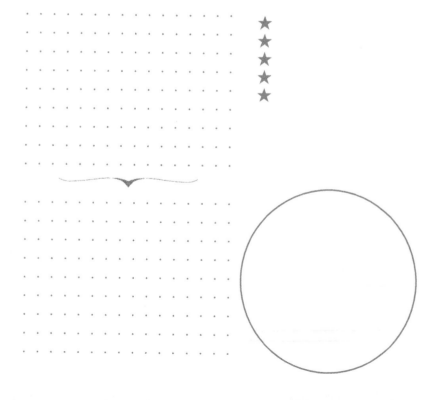

# SEVEN OF PENTACLES

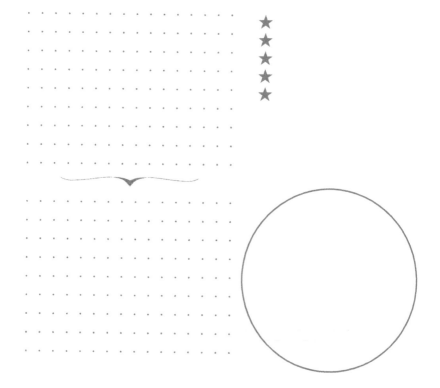

★
★
★
★
★

# EIGHT OF PENTACLES

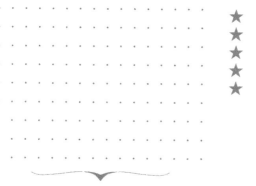

★
★
★
★
★

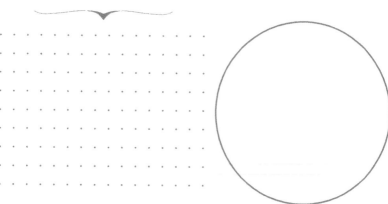

★
★
★
★
★

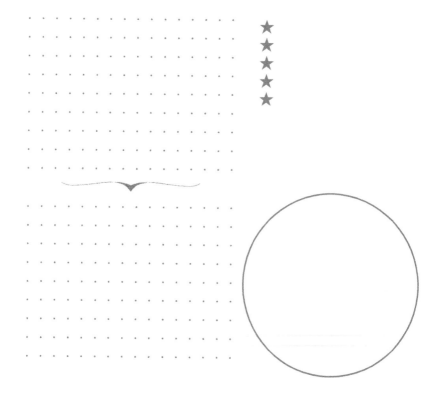

# TEN OF PENTACLES

★
★★
★★
★★
★

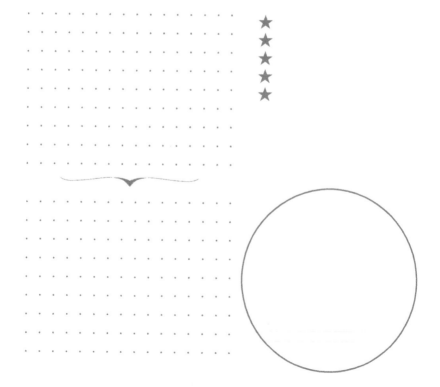

# SUIT OF SWORDS

*Other names include: Blades, Knives, Spades*

# SUIT OF SWORDS

# SUIT OF SWORDS

# SUIT OF SWORDS

# ACE OF SWORDS

★
★
★
★
★

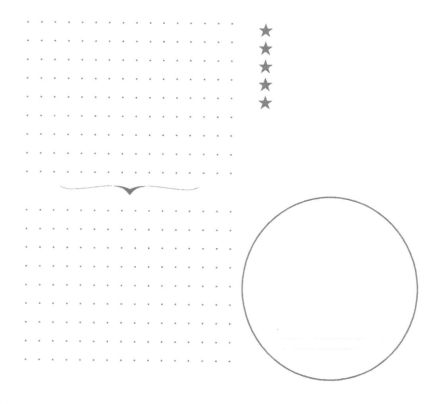

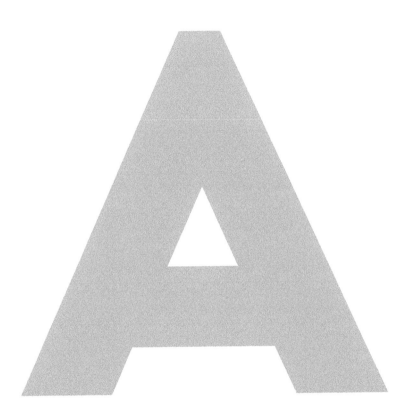

# TWO OF SWORDS

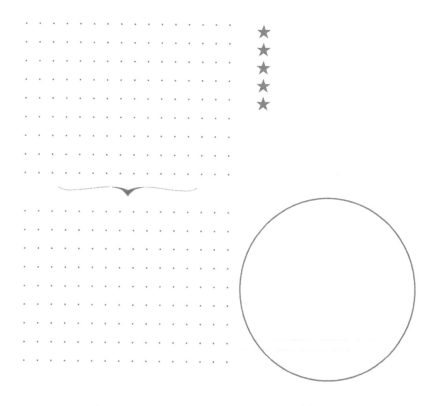

# THREE OF SWORDS

★
★
★
★
★

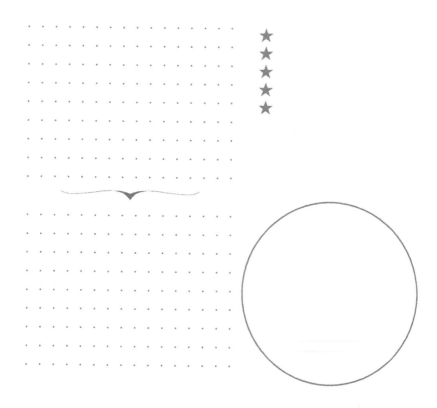

# FOUR OF SWORDS

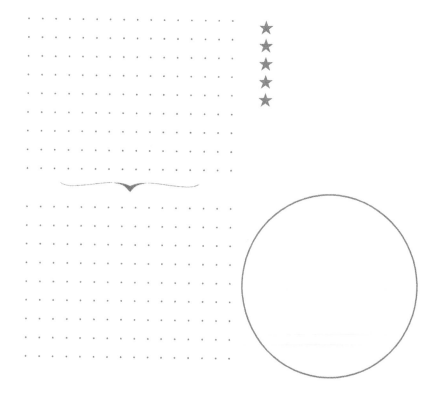

★
★
★
★
★

# FIVE OF SWORDS

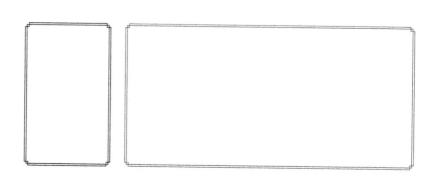

★
★
★
★
★

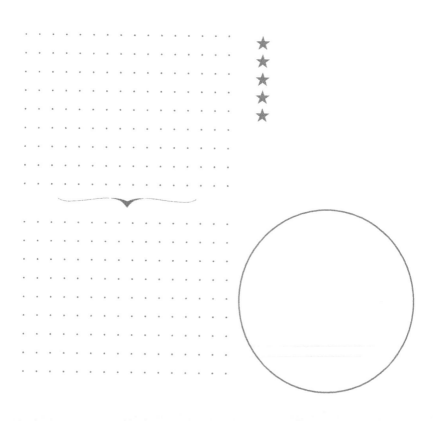

# SIX OF SWORDS

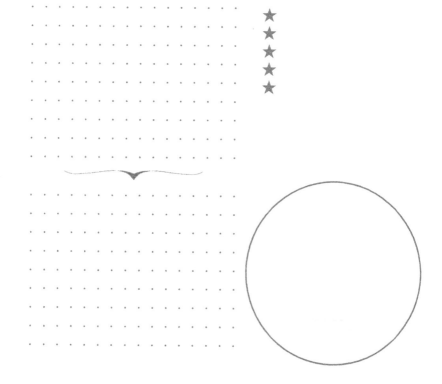

# SEVEN OF SWORDS

★
★
★
★
★

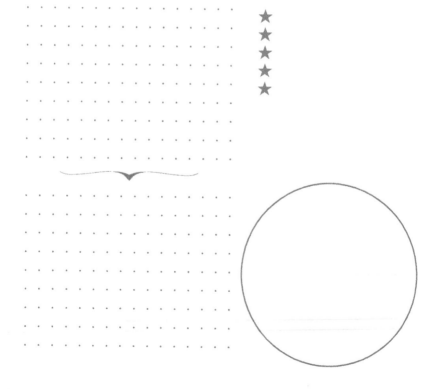

# EIGHT OF SWORDS

★
★
★
★
★

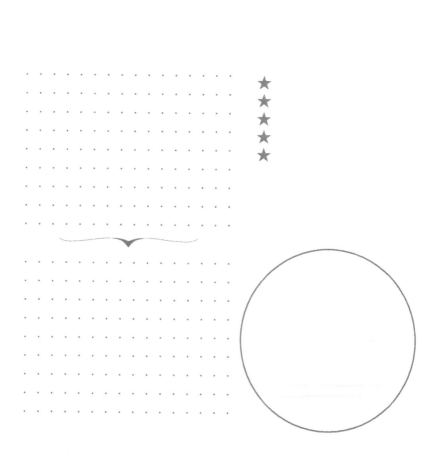

# NINE OF SWORDS

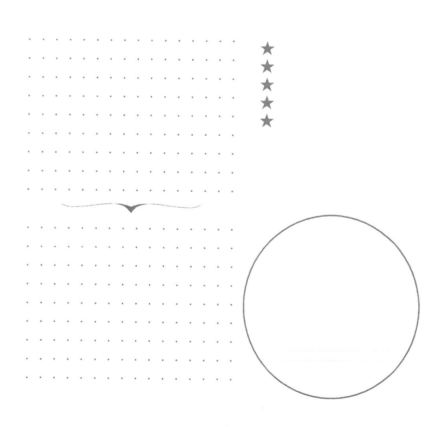

# TEN OF SWORDS

★
★★
★★★
★★★★
★★★★★

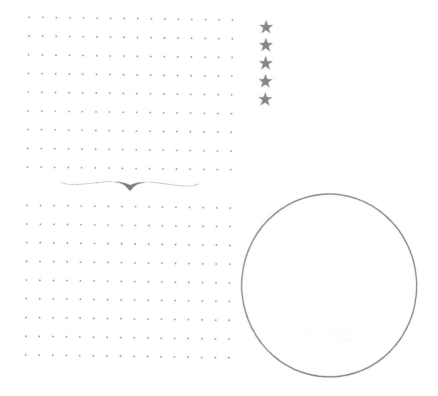

# SUIT OF WANDS

*Other names include: Rods, Staves, Clubs*

# SUIT OF WANDS

# SUIT OF WANDS

# SUIT OF WANDS

# ACE OF WANDS

★
★
★
★
★

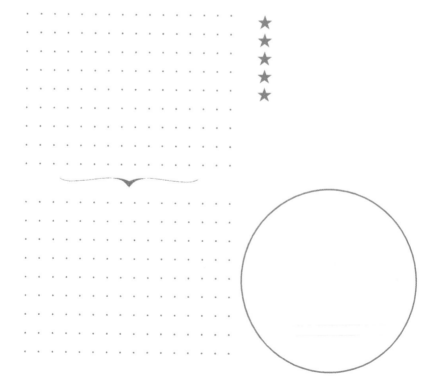

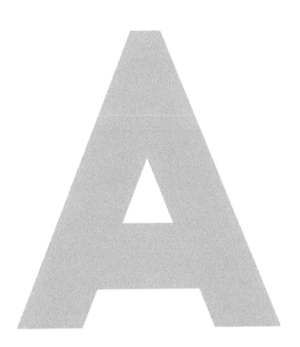

# TWO OF WANDS

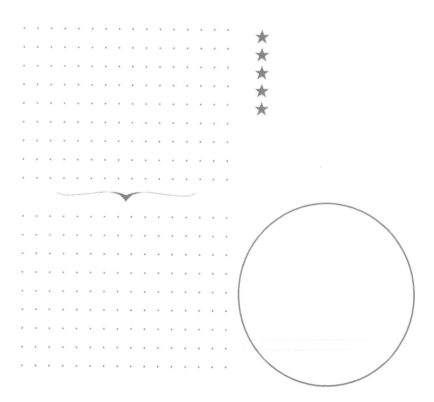

# THREE OF WANDS

★
★
★
★
★

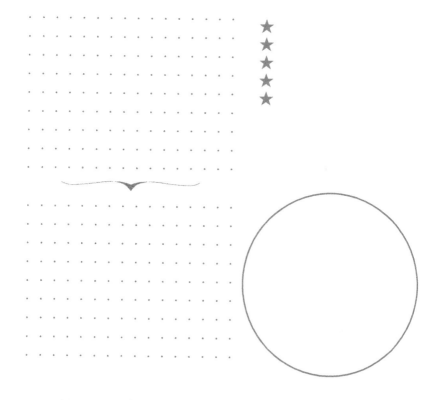

# FOUR OF WANDS

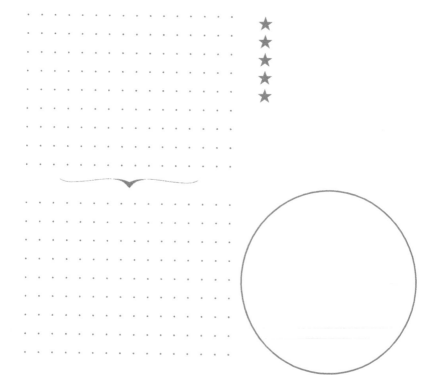

★
★
★
★
★

# FIVE OF WANDS

★
★
★
★
★

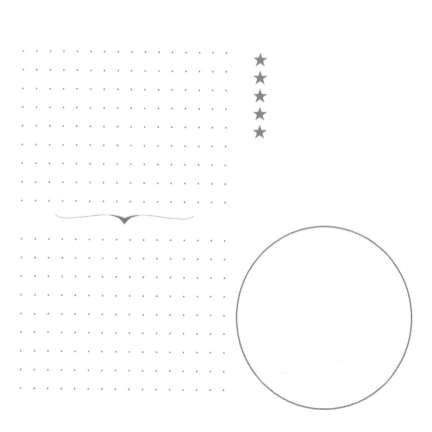

# SIX OF WANDS

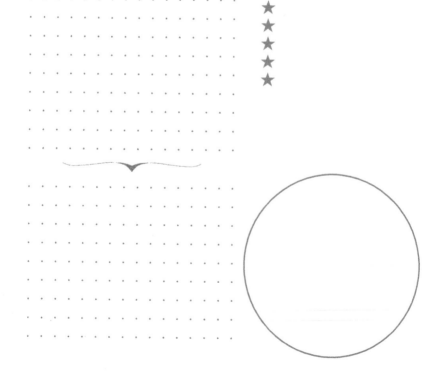

★
★
★
★
★

# SEVEN OF WANDS

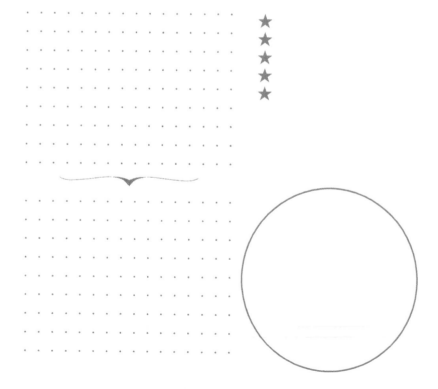

# EIGHT OF WANDS

★
★
★
★
★

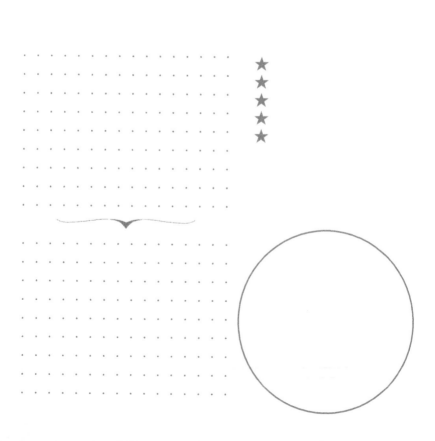

# NINE OF WANDS

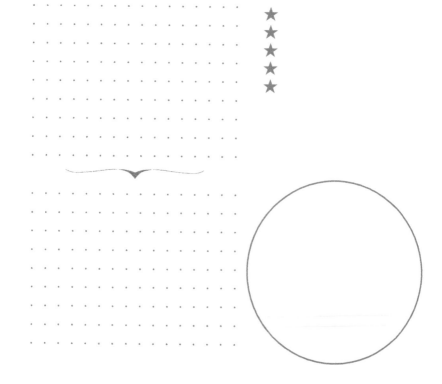

# TEN OF WANDS

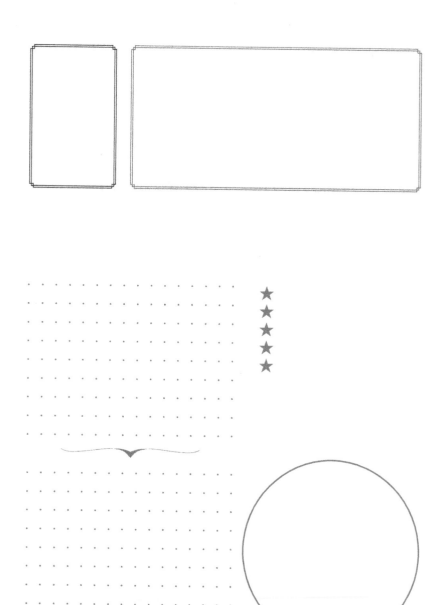

★
★
★
★
★

# COURT CARDS
## Pages, Knights, Queens & Kings

# COURT CARDS

# COURT CARDS

# OURT CARDS

# PAGE OF CUPS

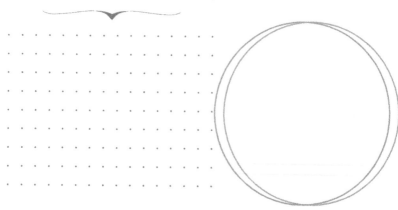

# KNIGHT OF CUPS

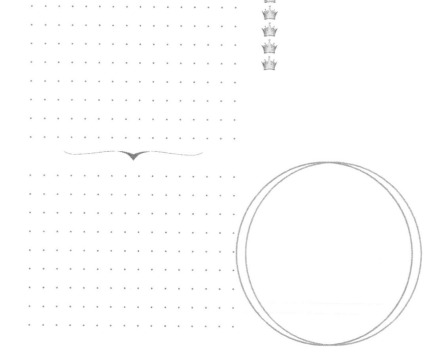

KN

# KN

# QUEEN OF CUPS

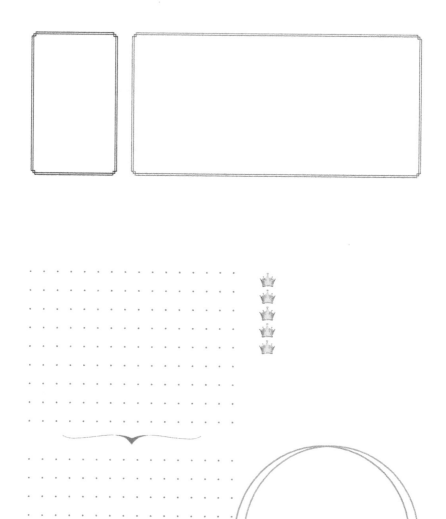

# KING OF CUPS

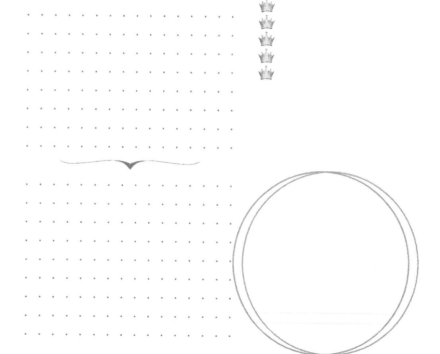

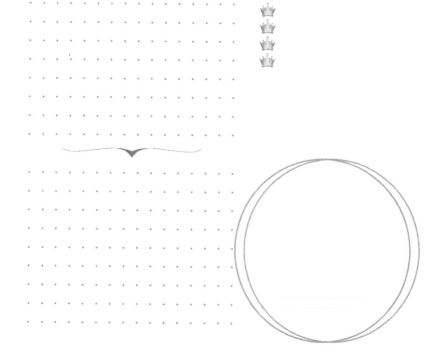

# KNIGHT OF PENTACLES

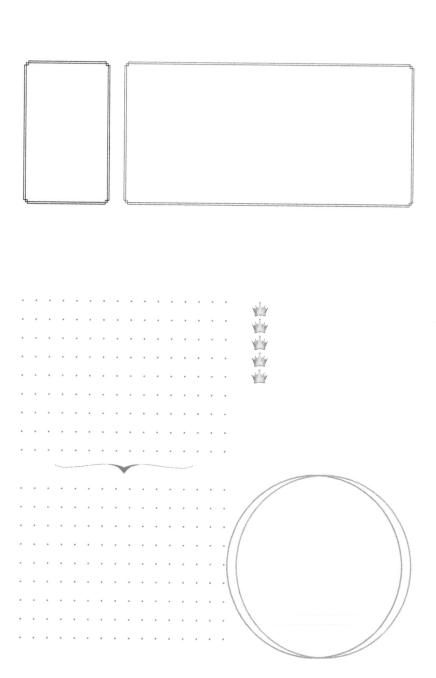

KN

# KN

# QUEEN OF PENTACLES

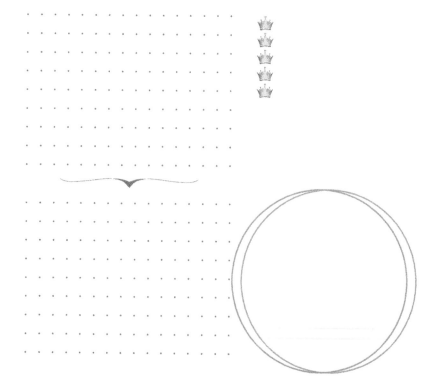

# KING OF PENTACLES

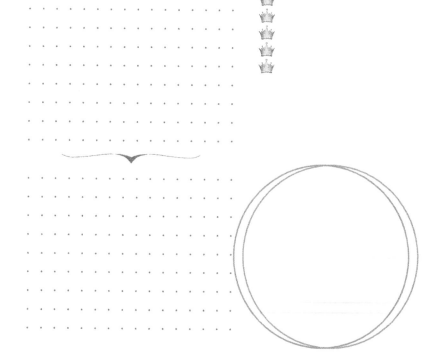

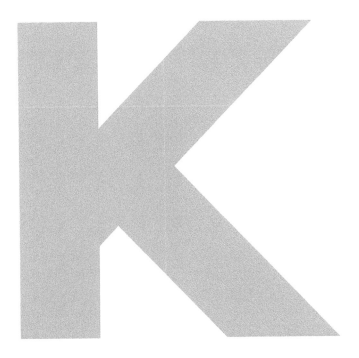

# PAGE OF SWORDS

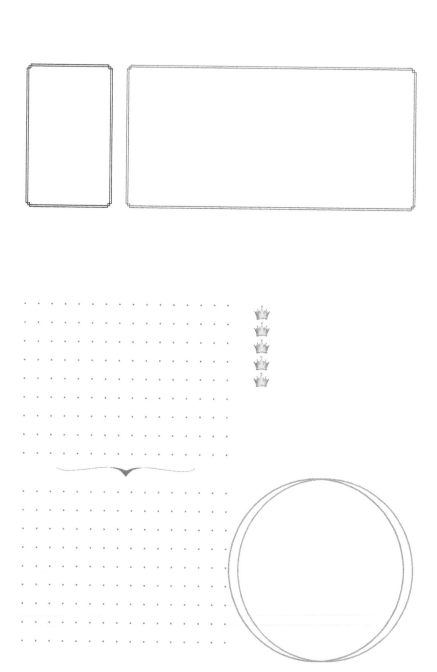

# KNIGHT OF SWORDS

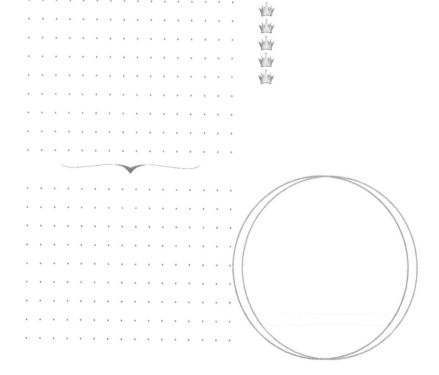

KN

KN

# QUEEN OF SWORDS

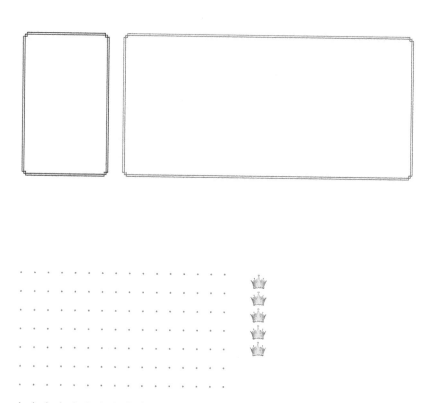

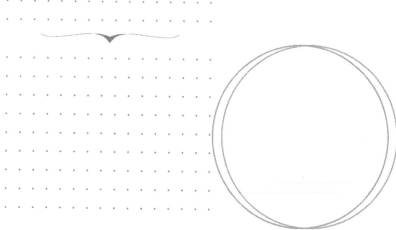

# KING OF SWORDS

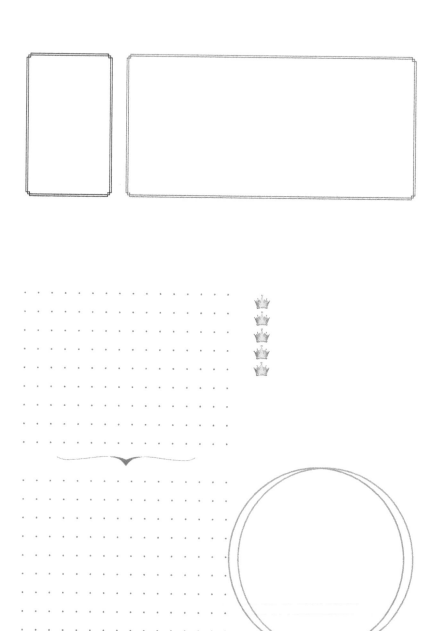

# K

# PAGE OF WANDS

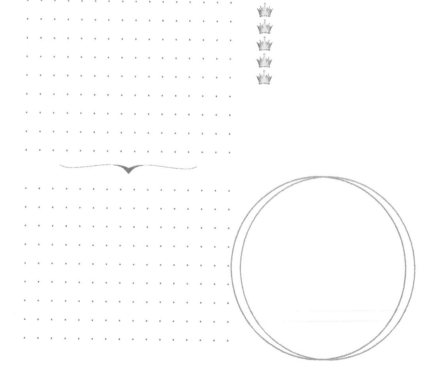

# KNIGHT OF WANDS

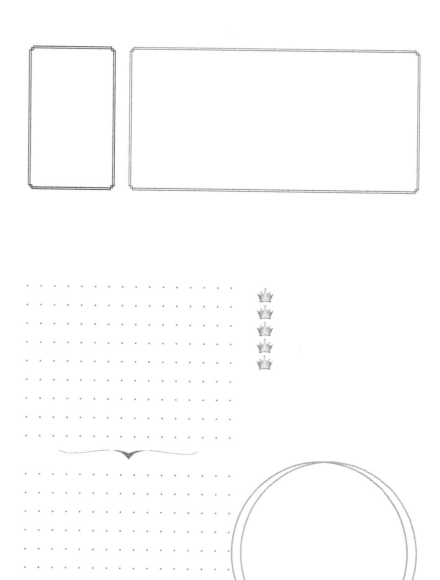

KN

KN

# QUEEN OF WANDS

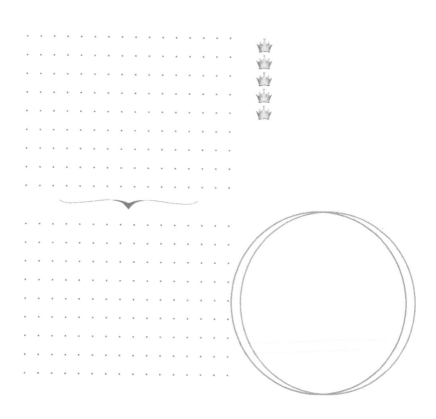

# KING OF WANDS

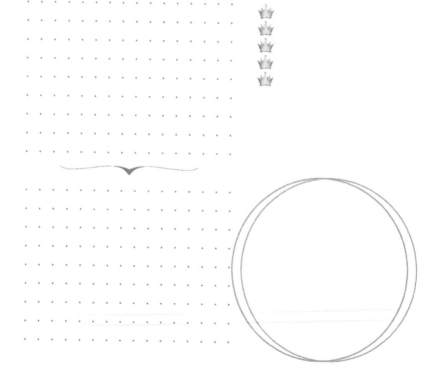

# The End!

## of all 78 cards

&

Still to come

*Lots more pages ahead for creating, designing and writing*

# SECTIONS

- Spreads
- Card Combinations
- Tarot Decks
- Other Decks
- Books
- Podcasts
- Websites
- Social Media
- Courses
- Notes

# SPREADS

Tarot readers often use a "spread" to help answer questions.

The idea is that each position in the spread represents a question or statement. The tarot card(s) positioned in each spot, gives the reader insights into the answers.

A popular spread contains three cards. Here are some examples:-

'Past' 'Present' & 'Future'
'Strength' 'Weakness' & Advice
'What to do' 'What not to do' & "What to continue'
'Situation' 'Action' & 'Outcome'
'Mind' 'Body' & 'Spirit'
'Option 1' 'Option 2' & 'How to choose'
'You' 'Them' & 'Us'

Find spreads you like & pop them here, or go *CRAZY*
& invent your own

# CARD COMBINATIONS

*You may notice card combos that come up time and time again - here is a place to capture those meanings!*

*The Chariot & Justice could indicate a Speeding Ticket*

_____

_____

_____

_____

_____

_____

_____

_____

_____

_____

_____

_____

_____

_____

_____

_____

_____

_____

# CARD COMBINATIONS

_____
_____
_____
_____
_____
_____
_____
_____
_____
_____
_____
_____
_____
_____
_____
_____
_____
_____
_____
_____
_____
_____
_____

# CARD COMBINATIONS

---
---
---
---
---
---
---
---
---
---
---
---
---
---
---
---
---
---
---
---
---
---
---
---
---
---

# CARD COMBINATIONS

_____
_____
_____
_____
_____
_____
_____
_____
_____
_____
_____
_____
_____
_____
_____
_____
_____
_____
_____
_____
_____
_____
_____
_____
_____
_____

# TAROT DECKS

*For ones I have.... and ones I want!*

_____ ☐
_____ ☐
_____ ☐
_____ ☐
_____ ☐
_____ ☐
_____ ☐
_____ ☐
_____ ☐
_____ ☐
_____ ☐
_____ ☐
_____ ☐
_____ ☐
_____ ☐
_____ ☐
_____ ☐
_____ ☐
_____ ☐
_____ ☐

# TAROT DECKS

_____ ☐
_____ ☐
_____ ☐
_____ ☐
_____ ☐
_____ ☐
_____ ☐
_____ ☐
_____ ☐
_____ ☐
_____ ☐
_____ ☐
_____ ☐
_____ ☐
_____ ☐
_____ ☐
_____ ☐
_____ ☐
_____ ☐
_____ ☐
_____ ☐
_____ ☐
_____ ☐

# TAROT DECKS

_____ ☐
_____ ☐
_____ ☐
_____ ☐
_____ ☐
_____ ☐
_____ ☐
_____ ☐
_____ ☐
_____ ☐
_____ ☐
_____ ☐
_____ ☐
_____ ☐
_____ ☐
_____ ☐
_____ ☐
_____ ☐
_____ ☐
_____ ☐
_____ ☐
_____ ☐
_____ ☐
_____ ☐

# TAROT DECKS

☐
☐
☐
☐
☐
☐
☐
☐
☐
☐
☐
☐
☐
☐
☐
☐
☐
☐
☐
☐
☐
☐

# OTHER DECKS

*For ones I have…. and ones I want!*

_____ ☐
_____ ☐
_____ ☐
_____ ☐
_____ ☐
_____ ☐
_____ ☐
_____ ☐
_____ ☐
_____ ☐
_____ ☐
_____ ☐
_____ ☐
_____ ☐
_____ ☐
_____ ☐
_____ ☐
_____ ☐
_____ ☐
_____ ☐
_____ ☐
_____ ☐

# OTHER DECKS

# BOOKS

*For ones I have.... and ones I want!*

# BOOKS

# BOOKS

# BOOKS

# PODCASTS

*For ones I have... and ones I want to try!*

_____

_____

_____

_____

_____

_____

_____

_____

_____

_____

_____

_____

_____

_____

_____

_____

_____

_____

_____

_____

_____

# PODCASTS

# PODCASTS

_____
_____
_____
_____
_____
_____
_____
_____
_____
_____
_____
_____
_____
_____
_____
_____
_____
_____
_____
_____
_____
_____
_____
_____

# PODCASTS

# WEBSITES

*For ones I have... and ones I want to try!*

WWW. _____
WWW. _____
WWW. _____
WWW. _____
WWW. _____
WWW. _____
WWW. _____
WWW. _____
WWW. _____
WWW. _____
WWW. _____
WWW. _____
WWW. _____
WWW. _____
WWW. _____
WWW. _____
WWW. _____
WWW. _____
WWW. _____
WWW. _____

# WEBSITES

WWW. _____

WWW. _____

WWW. _____

WWW. _____

WWW. _____

WWW. _____

WWW. _____

WWW. _____

WWW. _____

WWW. _____

WWW. _____

WWW. _____

WWW. _____

WWW. _____

WWW. _____

WWW. _____

WWW. _____

WWW. _____

WWW. _____

WWW. _____

WWW. _____

# WEBSITES

WWW. _____
WWW. _____
WWW. _____
WWW. _____
WWW. _____
WWW. _____
WWW. _____
WWW. _____
WWW. _____
WWW. _____
WWW. _____
WWW. _____
WWW. _____
WWW. _____
WWW. _____
WWW. _____
WWW. _____
WWW. _____
WWW. _____
WWW. _____
WWW. _____

# WEBSITES

WWW. _____

WWW. _____

WWW. _____

WWW. _____

WWW. _____

WWW. _____

WWW. _____

WWW. _____

WWW. _____

WWW. _____

WWW. _____

WWW. _____

WWW. _____

WWW. _____

WWW. _____

WWW. _____

WWW. _____

WWW. _____

WWW. _____

WWW. _____

WWW. _____

WWW. _____

# SOCIAL MEDIA

*For ones I love... and ones I want to explore!*

_____    _____
_____    _____
_____    _____
_____    _____
_____    _____
_____    _____
_____    _____
_____    _____
_____    _____
_____    _____
_____    _____
_____    _____
_____    _____
_____    _____
_____    _____
_____    _____
_____    _____

# SOCIAL MEDIA

_____    _____
_____    _____
_____    _____
_____    _____
_____    _____
_____    _____
_____    _____
_____    _____
_____    _____
_____    _____
_____    _____
_____    _____
_____    _____
_____    _____
_____    _____
_____    _____
_____    _____
_____    _____
_____    _____
_____    _____
_____    _____

# SOCIAL MEDIA

_____   _____
_____   _____
_____   _____
_____   _____
_____   _____
_____   _____
_____   _____
_____   _____
_____   _____
_____   _____
_____   _____
_____   _____
_____   _____
_____   _____
_____   _____
_____   _____
_____   _____
_____   _____
_____   _____
_____   _____
_____   _____
_____   _____

# SOCIAL MEDIA

_____   _____
_____   _____
_____   _____
_____   _____
_____   _____
_____   _____
_____   _____
_____   _____
_____   _____
_____   _____
_____   _____
_____   _____
_____   _____
_____   _____
_____   _____
_____   _____
_____   _____
_____   _____
_____   _____
_____   _____
_____   _____
_____   _____

# COURSES

| Name | Username | Password |
|------|----------|----------|
| | | |
| | | |
| | | |
| | | |
| | | |
| | | |
| | | |
| | | |
| | | |
| | | |
| | | |
| | | |
| | | |
| | | |
| | | |
| | | |
| | | |
| | | |
| | | |

# COURSES

| _Name_ | _Username_ | _Password_ |
|--------|------------|------------|
| | | |
| | | |
| | | |
| | | |
| | | |
| | | |
| | | |
| | | |
| | | |
| | | |
| | | |
| | | |
| | | |
| | | |
| | | |
| | | |
| | | |
| | | |
| | | |

# NOTES

# NOTES

_____
_____
_____
_____
_____
_____
_____
_____
_____
_____
_____
_____
_____
_____
_____
_____
_____
_____
_____
_____
_____
_____
_____
_____
_____
_____
_____

# NOTES

# NOTES

_____
_____
_____
_____
_____
_____
_____
_____
_____
_____
_____
_____
_____
_____
_____
_____
_____
_____
_____
_____
_____
_____
_____
_____
_____
_____

# NOTES

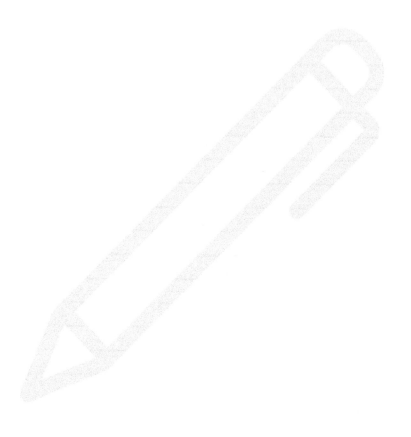

# NOTES

_____
_____
_____
_____
_____
_____
_____
_____
_____
_____
_____
_____
_____
_____
_____
_____
_____
_____
_____
_____
_____
_____
_____
_____
_____
_____
_____
_____

# NOTES

# NOTES

# NOTES

# NOTES

_____

_____

_____

_____

_____

_____

_____

_____

_____

_____

_____

_____

_____

_____

_____

_____

_____

_____

_____

_____

_____

_____

_____

_____

# NOTES

# NOTES

# NOTES

# NOTES

_____
_____
_____
_____
_____
_____
_____
_____
_____
_____
_____
_____
_____
_____
_____
_____
_____
_____
_____
_____
_____
_____
_____
_____
_____
_____
_____